D0568870

Beautiful
Alaska®

Featuring Ed Cooper and Bob Spring Photography

Text: Paul M. Lewis

Design: Patrick H. Kolb

Published by Beautiful America Publishing Company
9775 S.W. Commerce Circle
Wilsonville, Oregon 97070
First Published November, 1977
Second Edition April, 1984

Copyright © 1977 by Beautiful America Publishing Company
Printed in the United States of America
ISBN 0-915796-14-7 (hardback)
ISBN 0-89802-413-7 (paperback)

CONTENTS

The Watery Highway

It slides a long, skinny finger down along the northwest coast of the continent. The finger is very wet, and not very solid, as a proper finger should be. This is southeastern Alaska, the "Panhandle," the "Inside Passage," or, as the mapmakers would have it, the Alexander Archipelago. From Ketchikan at the southern end to Skagway, 400 miles to the north, the 60-mile-wide archipelago is crowded with about 11,000 big and little islands (if you count all those that barely clear the water at high tide). Some of the islands are so squeezed together that they afford only a hairsbreadth passage to the big ferries and other cruise ships that wiggle their way through the narrow straits, to the intense delight of their passengers. One especially tight channel, Wrangell Narrows, is between Kupreanof and Mitkof islands. The trip through the Narrows, on the run between Wrangell and Petersburg, calls for some artful teasing by ships' captains. Another such perilous passage occurs between Chichagof and Baranof islands on the way to Sitka. The drama is intensified when the route is negotiated at night; marker lights flash in the channel, and varicolored searchlights from the ship play over forest vegetation that seems at times only an arm's length away from the vessel.

The prickly thrills of scraping through such bottlenecks yield to other kinds of equally enjoyable adventures during travel through the archipelago. This part of Alaska may lay legitimate claim to that overworked descriptive "spectacular." It has so many kinds of spectacle that the mind boggles at their complexity. The endless waterways come in an infinite variety of shapes and sizes. One has only begun to tell the story by classifying them as bays, fjords, inlets, channels, straits, and sounds. The islands they touch are mostly uninhabited and even, in some cases, unexplored. Most of the 50,000 population (20 per cent native) is concentrated in the 17 or so towns of the archipelago. Juneau (soon to lose its status as state capital) leads the list with about 18,000 inhabitants. The complex watery canyons themselves were cut by glaciers.

The land is not just "there" in southeastern Alaska. It has awesome presence wherever a traveler looks, whether he is taking a water or air route. Because the islands are the tips of submerged mountains, they rise abruptly from the water, their sharp outlines the result of sculpturing by glaciers that have advanced and retreated over eons of time. The glaciers come into the picture north of Juneau, their blue-white rivers of ice moving slowly down from icefields on both sides of Lynn Canal north to Skagway.

All of the archipelago is in a relatively mild climatic area with abundant rain (averaging about 100 inches annually), so is heavily forested. Except for the towns, the whole region is in the Tongass National Forest, the largest national forest in the United States. Its spruce and hemlocks are one of the basic means of livelihood for Alaskans who live here. The mountainous slopes of the "Passage" seem to be cloaked in green velvet, so dense are the stands of timber on them. The thousands of streams fostered by the steep terrain and melting glaciers are rich salmon spawning grounds, so both sports and commercial fishing are important activities.

In the waters and the air of the archipelago are some of the more freewheeling members of nature's mammal and avian families. Cruise ship passengers can usually count on sightings of porpoises, whales, killer whales, sea lions, and seals. And here is the last region left where the bald eagle still lives in significant numbers (about 20,000). This symbol of power, majesty, and grace is often observed in the skies above southeastern Alaska.

Juneau and the other towns of the Panhandle so far have managed to avoid intruding to a harmful extent on the natural beauty of their sea and mountain environment. The other two "big cities" are Ketchikan (11,500) and Sitka (6,500). Each of the communities of southeastern Alaska has its own personality and some, like Ketchikan, still have the flavor of their Indian beginnings. Ketchikan started out as a Tlingit fishing village, and for many years after it became a town, salmon fishing and canning was its chief industry. When salmon declined, lumber moved in as the number one means of livelihood. A town on an island (Revillagigedo), Ketchikan's main link with the rest of the world is by air. Wrangell, 89 miles up the narrows, is a waterfront community like Ketchikan. It was first a Russian fort (St. Dionysius) in 1834, then a British trading post in 1839 (Fort Stikine), finally emerging as an American military post (Fort Wrangell) after the purchase of Alaska in 1867 by the United States. Indian civilization in the Ketchikan-Wrangell areas is memorialized by a large number of totem poles—originals and replicas—and evidenced in the petroglyphs on beach rocks.

Petersburg, 32 miles north of Wrangell, was founded by Norwegian fishermen, and is still populated mostly by their descendants. Fishing still provides the main livelihood, and a good one, too. Per capita income is one of the highest in the United States. Physically, Petersburg is a bit of Scandinavia in Alaska. Its fishing fleet clusters in the large harbor; one side of Main Street is the waterfront, where processing plants stand in Wrangell Narrows on tall pilings; and the houses are painted white.

Sitka is not just a town. It is history preserved in a community. Sitka was for long the headquarters of the Russian fur traders after Alexander Baranof founded it in 1799.

It became the capital of Russian America in 1806 and remained so until 1867, when the United Sates took possession of the town. The name, by the way, is adapted from a Tlingit Indian word meaning "by the sea." The Tlingits pronounced it with an "h," which may have sounded unseemly to ears other than theirs. Baranof built a magnificent castle on a site with a sweeping view of the town and the bay. This structure was replaced several times by other Russian-built castles, but the last burned in 1897. Castle Hill, where they stood, is now a national historical site. Sitka is located in one of southeast Alaska's most attractive settings. It has a backdrop of mountains, an island-dotted harbor, and a symmetrical extinct volcano, Mount Edgecumbe, a little out to sea. Some of the town's historic buildings were destroyed in a disastrous fire in 1966 but restoration of the most highly prized structure of all—St. Michael's Cathedral—is being undertaken.

Southeast Alaska's "metropolis" is Juneau, the state capital. Like Wrangell and Ketchikan it is spread out on a narrow ledge that clings to steep hillsides behind it, in this case massive Mount Juneau. Seen from the waters of deep Gastineau Channel, the town is hemmed in on the right by the steep sides of Mount Roberts. It has tall buildings as a state capital should. If the Borough of Juneau and City of Douglas across the channel are included, Juneau encompasses 3,180 square miles, making it the largest city in area in the United States. Eskimo, Indian, and Russian influences are given attention in Juneau's Alaska State Museum, and the city's colorful beginnings as a gold rush town are still evidenced by the ruins of mine structures on Mount Roberts and tailings from the Alaska-Juneau mine that form the south wall of the harbor. Just north of Juneau is the popular and accessible Mendenhall Glacier, 14 miles long and 4 miles wide. It presents an impressive face to water travelers, dipping down from the Juneau Icefield, just over the mountain wall. The icefield is an incredible 40-by-100-mile deepfreeze that spawns all the glaciers hereabouts.

The little village of Haines, toward the north end of Lynn Canal, has lots of history behind it. It started as an Indian village, then became a Chilkat trading post, a Presbyterian mission town, a placer gold mining site (at the turn of the century), and the takeoff point for the Dalton Trail, which led over the mountain passes to the Klondike gold fields of the Yukon. Haines is now the port on the Inside Passage that connects with the Alaska Highway and other points north.

Colorful Skagway sits between towering mountains at the northern end of the "protected" Inside Passage. The little gold rush boom town still looks much the same as it did during its heyday in 1897-98. The name, in Tlingit, means "end of the salt water," or "home of the north wind," depending on whose expertise you are the beneficiary of. During those brief and frantic times when it was the starting point for the gold rush trail over White Pass to Lake Bennett, the population was about 15,000. Now it's 850.

Passengers on the "Marine Highway" ferries and cruise ships that stop here are intrigued by the studied "Klondike" atmosphere, carefully preserved by the residents, nearly all of whom are in some way dependent on tourism for their living. Tourists still like to walk over the old Chilkoot Trail (with the help of a guide), or take the scenic train ride to Whitehorse in the Yukon over the narrow-gauge railroad that winds through the mountains over the same route followed by the '98 gold seekers. Skagway has lost its hustle and bustle but not its pioneer charm and friendly hospitality to visitors.

If the water wanderer through the Inside Passage turns west around Admiralty Island instead of heading for Skagway he will shortly enter Icy Strait, an arm of the "Passage" open to the sea, and an aptly named prelude to Glacier Bay National Park, in the northwest part of the Panhandle. What makes Glacier Bay so very special is the savage, primeval, elemental nature personified in its 20 or so colossal glaciers (16 tidal glaciers) whose leading edges set up a mighty thunder as they slide into the waters of the Bay; its wild, furious streams; its winds, its torrential rains, and its earthquakes. The National Park is 4,400 square miles of raw, natural power displayed on a grand scale.

Glacier Bay is special for another, and surprising, reason. It has been a bay for not much more than 100 years, its depths filled until the late 18th century by a tremendous wall of ice which we now call the Grand Pacific Glacier. There was no bay when George Vancouver picked his way through the ice of Icy Strait in the 1790s. But since then, the Grand Pacific has drawn back an amazing 70 miles to one of the Bay's heads, while other ice sheets have retreated to create the various arms of the Bay. Where land has been uncovered, spruce and hemlock forest grow and wildlife has become abundant. With protection as a national park, Glacier Bay's unique wilderness will exist for a long time to come as one of the jewels of southeast Alaska.

South Central Alaska

This part of Alaska has many of the attributes of the Panhandle, especially in the coastal stretches, although it is more subject to the sometimes violent moods of the Gulf of Alaska, to which its unprotected shores are exposed. But it is blessed, like the Archipelago, with abundant rain and comparatively mild temperatures, and parts of it are covered by great icefields and glaciers. It contains Alaska's most lofty mountain ranges, including the tallest peak on the continent, and huge areas of multivaried and abundant wildlife. It covers some 400 miles in an east-west direction, from the St. Elias Mountains in the east to the Alaska and Aleutian ranges where they rise in a generally north-south orientation west of Cook Inlet. Katmai National Park, at the top of the Alaska Peninsula, should be included, but the rest of the peninsula, bending west between the Bering Sea and the Pacific Ocean, really belongs to southwest Alaska. The northern boundary of south central Alaska is the Alaska Range, which stretches across to the Yukon and separates this region from the Interior. Where the north-south and east-west arms of the range meet is Denali National Park, a forest and mountain preserve that provides a protected setting for Mt. McKinley and some other giants.

At the risk of offending some of the critters who have put down stakes in Alaska's Interior, this richly endowed land-and-water area might be characterized as Alaska's heartland. It has rich fishing resources in its bays, inlets, and Prince William Sound; super-abundant wild animal life in its vast and thickly forested mountain ranges, especially on the Kenai Peninsula; the bountiful Matanuska Valley between the Chugach and Talkeetna mountains; and some of Alaska's major communities in terms of potential growth and importance: Anchorage, Valdez, Cordova, Whittier.

It's hard to decide where to begin a commentary on this complex region . Perhaps the most orderly way is to start in the east where a neck of land rises out of the northern tip of the panhandle. The Yakutat Bay area is really still southeastern Alaska, but since it is not part of the archipelago I have included it in this section. It has a mild climate, summer and winter, and is acclaimed by hunters and fishermen for the incredible bounty of fish and animal life there. Yakutat Bay is *the* fishing grounds for king salmon and provides rich harvests of shrimp and dungeness crab. This stretch of the Alaska coast also produces a seemingly infinite variety of bottom fish. Near the village of Yakutat the hunting is rewarding for stalkers of moose, bear, blacktail deer, and waterfowl.

The coastal crescent that starts at Yakutat is not known for its peaceful behavior. Lituya Bay, south of the town, was massively rearranged in one of Alaska's recent (1958) earthquakes when a whole mountainside crashed into the bay, creating a huge tidal wave that swept seaward, stripping most of the vegetation in its path. The height of the wave is still indicated by the bay's vegetation line. Speaking of big, the biggest glacier on the continent —Malaspina—can be seen at some distance from Yakutat. This coastal glacier covers more lateral area than the state of Rhode Island.

The mountain ranges that feed these and other glaciers are some of the most spectacular in North America. The Chugach Mountains are along the crescent, the Wrangells are just north of the Chugach, and the St. Elias range straddles the Alaska-Canada border. In this area are 16,390-foot Mount Blackburn, 16,237-foot Mount Sanford, and 18,008-foot Mount St. Elias. With icefields, unspoiled and rugged hills, wild rivers, and great roaming caribou herds, these massive ranges are in Wrangell-St. Elias National Park. Large numbers of large animals besides caribou range over these mountains: grizzly bears, black bears, moose, and wolves. That shy dweller on the high mountain slopes, the Dall sheep, sometimes grows to great size here.

The Copper River drains this area. Its watershed and those of other wild streams hereabout are havens and nesting areas for some of the earth's hard-pressed avian wildlife: trumpeter swans, bald eagles, and peregrine falcons. The waterfowl breed here in great numbers. Like Yakutat Bay down the coast, the Copper River Delta has a prodigious salmon run. Towns or other evidences of human intrusion are almost nonexistent. Tiny Chitina, at the confluence of the Chitina and Copper rivers, has about 35 houses. It is on a 35-mile scenic road that takes off from the Richardson Highway, Alaska route 4 that starts at Valdez on Prince William Sound. Chitina is an historic place, with a copper mining background. Earlier in the century it and McCarthy, 63 miles farther along the road, were centers of copper mining for the Kennicott Copper Company. McCarthy is now nearly a ghost town, its mines abandoned. But it still welcomes the adventurous explorer who appreciates a nearly untouched spectacular wilderness enough to risk traveling the primitive road from Chitina. This wilderness is now in danger because of the state's plans for a paved highway out of Cordova to connect with the Richardson Highway.

Cordova, farther along the coastal crescent at the east end of Prince William Sound, still has no road connections to other Alaska points. But is is served by air and by Marine Highway ferries from Valdez and Whittier. It is a fishing and logging town whose character may undergo some changes as nearby Valdez becomes more and more important in its role of oil pipeline terminus. Valdez now has a few more people than

Paradise Peak on the Kenai Peninsula – E. Cooper

(Following) View from Blackberry Ridge near Juneau – E. Cooper

Lena Cove about 15 miles north of Juneau—E. Cooper

A tundra pond in Denali National Park – E. Cooper

A mountain stream near Valdez – E. Cooper

Tlingit totem poles near Ketchikan – B. Spring

14

(Following) Byron Glacier near Portage . . . the source-waters of Byron Creek – E. Cooper

Wild sweet pea – B. Spring

Wild geranium – B. Spring

(Opposite) Mt. McKinley – E. Cooper

Ferns in a rainforest near Juneau — E. Cooper

Gold rush cabins near Fairbanks – B. Spring

Sourdough cabin at Kantishna – E. Cooper

Mt. Sanford and Grizzly Lake in the Wrangell Mountains – E. Cooper

The Denali Highway winds over foothill country a few miles west of Paxson – B. Spring

Tundra and foothills near Denali National Park – B. Spring

(Following) Portage Glacier and Portage Lake near Anchorage – E. Cooper

Nome Eskimos – B. Spring

Stellar sea lions bask on Sea Lion Rock, Amak Island—B. Spring

Mt. Brooks in Denali National Park – E. Cooper

Sunrise in Juneau Icefield – E. Cooper

(Following) Mt. McKinley and Wonder Lake – E. Cooper

31

The small-boat harbor near the end of Homer Spit – E. Cooper

Wolf Cove in Glacier Bay National Park – B. Spring

Dwarf fireweed near Byron Peak – E. Cooper

View from the Klondike Loop Highway – B. Spring

Fireweed near Tiekel—E. Cooper

Juneau's Auke Bay—E. Cooper

40

Turnagain Flats, Cook Inlet – E. Cooper

A dairy farm in Mananuska Valley – B. Spring

Bridal Veil Falls in Keystone Canyon near Valdez – E. Cooper

Awesome Peak in the Chugach Mountains—E. Cooper

Mt. Sanford viewed from Grizzly Lake – E. Cooper

Colorful Rainbow Mountain near Paxon — E. Cooper

Mt. Carpathian southwest of Whittier – E. Cooper

Chena River – E. Cooper

Moonlight Campground on the Alaska Highway—B. Spring

Mt. Drum viewed from the Copper River – E. Cooper

51

Jigging for tomcod – B. Spring

Johns Hopkins Inlet in Glacier Bay National Park – B. Spring

Columbia Glacier in Prince William Sound–E. Cooper

Whitestone Narrows of Peril Straits – B. Spring

Cordova and will probably become much bigger when the oil starts to flow and the tankers start carrying it to the lower forty-nine. These two Prince William Sound communities have had their troubles in recent memory. In 1964 both were hit by an earthquake, Valdez much more severely. Cordova's harbor sustained extensive damage, but much of Valdez was destroyed, and 33 persons killed. The present Valdez was entirely rebuilt, on a new site, after the quake. It is in a beautiful setting, surrounded by tall mountains, and possessing an attractive small-boat harbor.

Prince William Sound is a place of extravagant beauty much in the manner of the Inside Passage in southeastern Alaska. It has mountains and glaciers and fjords throughout its long, convoluted coastline. One of Alaska's more showoffy glaciers attracts the attention of visitors—especially ship passengers—to this area. This is the Columbia Glacier, between Whittier and Valdez. It will obligingly "calve" icebergs into the waters of the sound when a ship's captain toots his whistle. Whittier Glacier and those of College Fjord (each glacier named for a college) are accessible to many kinds of animal life, including human.

The next step over to the west brings into focus the Kenai Peninsula, whose northeast shores form the western arm of Prince William Sound. The peninsula is another one of south central Alaska's wilderness spectaculars, probably more renowned than almost any other area of the world as a paradise for sportsmen and big game hunters, offering unrivaled opportunities for experiencing nature in stunning surroundings unspoiled by human improvements. For all its wild character, the peninsula is just south of Alaska's biggest city—Anchorage. The topography is as varied as one could wish. The Chugach Mountains form a massive wall of peaks down the eastern side while the western length is largely wooded plateau country interlaced with an enormous number of lakes and streams. In addition to supporting huge bands of the world's biggest moose (in Kenai National Moose Range), the western side harbors the enormous brown bear and other wild specimens of more modest size, including Dall sheep and goats. There is some development on Kenai, but so far it is modest and unobtrusive. This stunning setting is all the more attractive because of its mild weather, fostered by the Japan current, that marvelous, warm river in the Pacific Ocean that flows northeast past Japan.

The towns of the peninsula, like most Alaskan communities, are small, but their easy road and rail access from Anchorage plus the inevitable push of "progress" may change things before long. One small sign of this is the Alyeska ski resort just north of Turnagain Arm at the top of the peninsula near Anchorage. The more visitors, the more "facilities." The road from Anchorage to Seward, a town on the east peninsula coast, has many delightful aspects. In waterfall areas that skirt Turnagain Arm, myriad little cascades fed by mountain snows or heavy rainfall flash down the slopes in exuberant abandon. Their contribution to the beauty of the scene extends beyond their own good looks. They help provide the moist climate needed by certain wildflowers, such as the wild snapdragon (also called monkey flower) that gives a yellow accent to the green and gray foliage here.

The glaciers are numerous, too, in this northern neck of the peninsula. One of the best known of these is Portage Glacier, now included in a Forest Service recreational area with its own campgrounds. This way, the glacier and glacial lake into which it spits icebergs can be experienced and enjoyed at first hand. Those persons who really want to experience nature at first hand and who have the determination and stamina may do this by traveling the Resurrection Pass Hiking Trail that takes off from the community of Hope, a former gold mining town on the south shore of Turnagain Arm. The trail is 40 miles long and follows Resurrection Creek up the valley and over the pass (2,600 feet) to the Kenai River. On the trail one may encounter the huge and sometimes dangerous, brown bear, as well as the small, and always aggravating, mosquito. The former are merely hungry; the latter are ravenous.

In the area of Seward is another awesome Kenai spectacle, the Harding Icefield. This enormous ice mass covers more than 850 square miles. Seward's Resurrection Bay has a splendid ice-free harbor and excellent sports fishing. Stellar sea lions, whales, and porpoises populate the islands and waters of the bay, while bear, mountain goat, and Dall sheep inhabit the shores.

The west side of the Kenai Peninsula, isolated and remote, is experiencing the beginnings of an economic boom. Alaska Highway 1 (Sterling Highway) now connects the towns, all growing a little with the arrival of enterprises other than the former mainstay, fishing. Oil and natural gas wells are contributing to the economy and could change the whole character of the peninsula if even more reserves are discovered.

But for now, the road to Soldotna, Kenai, and Homer is a pathway through wild and fascinating landscape whose variety gives it the advantage of being a miniature Alaska all by itself. Kenai Lake, near the junction of the Anchorage-Seward highway and Highway 1, is surrounded by ridges of the Chugach National Forest, on whose slopes Dall sheep are a common sight. Many other fishing lakes and rivers are part of the scenery here. Also in this general area is the Kenai National Wildlife Range, where the moose roam in large numbers on more than 1.5 million acres set aside for their preservation. The town of Soldotna to the west provides access to the Wildlife Range. It is also one of the important communities of the peninsula although established quite recently (in the 1940s) compared with Kenai and Homer, the other two sizeable towns on the Cook Inlet side of the Peninsula. Soldotna connects with the other two, its location at the Sterling Highway-Kenai Road junction being the reason it became a town in the first place. A more esthetic reason for its importance is the magnificent view it commands of snow-covered Aleutian Range volcanoes about 60 miles away across Cook Inlet. Soldotna's setting is heavily forested and laced with many streams. The visitor has the opportunity of seeing some of the area's abundant wildlife by taking a canoe trip through the wilderness where they live. One of the bonuses of visiting places like this in late summer or early fall is the diversified menu of berries offered to the picker. The same berries are also offered to the bears in these parts, so one should choose a berry bush that either has not yet provided, or is not at the moment providing, dinner for one of the large and shaggy set.

Kenai is the peninsula's biggest town. Its 4,000 residents account for a quarter of the entire Kenai Peninsula human population. If every individual of every species of animal life here had a vote, the people types would find themselves in a very tiny minority party. But the town of Kenai, where people *do* have a vote, is a sort of boom town, with an important Russian and Indian historical background. Oil is providing the boom, although fishing is still an important industry. But Kenai was an Indian village before it became a Russian fort (in 1791), the second permanent town established by them in Alaska. The Russian influence is still visible in the historic Russian Orthodox Church. The American contribution is still visible in Fort Kenay, nearby the town, built by the U.S. Army in 1869. One of Kenai's important present-day roles is as a gateway to all that peninsular wilderness that has become so popular as an Alaskan recreational area. Standing on the eastern shore of Cook Inlet, it has high ground with a sweeping view of the inlet; the giant volcanoes, Mount Redoubt and Mount Iliamna, on the far shore, and (in spring and early summer) great white beluga whales which come to feed in the Kenai River.

Homer, once all alone on the western tip of the Kenai Peninsula, is getting a touristy gleam in its eye these days. The enterprising residents are boosting it as Alaska's "Shangri-la," and with some good reason. It's generously endowed with marvelous scenery, has a mild climate, and a splendid deepwater bay (Kachemak Bay) that reaches up into the peninsula for 30 miles and separates Homer from the wild, glacier-covered Kenai Mountains on the south point of the peninsula.

Kodiak Island is actually the main land mass in a group of islands that lie alongside the northern Alaska Peninsula, and south-southwest of Kenai Peninsula. It is another land of superlatives, one of which is descriptive of the island's biggest and best-known resident, the Kodiak brown bear. The gigantic beast is the biggest carnivore in North America, reaching 1,200 pounds. Unfortunately for him, the wiliest carnivore in North America is hunting him to such an extent that fewer and fewer specimens are attaining their full growth. People have known about the bear for a long time—Russians established Kodiak, the first non-native settlement in Alaska, in 1792. The town of Kodiak is older than Sitka, and was the capital of Russian Alaska until the latter town took over the title in 1804. The oldest Russian building in Alaska is in Kodiak; it is now a museum housing Russian and Aleut artifacts. Much of the town, along the wooded shores of Chiniak Bay, was destroyed by a seismic wave that followed the '64 earthquake, but it has been rebuilt with careful attention to its Russian and Indian heritage. The king crab has become the mainstay of the island's most important industry: fishing, particularly shellfish, salmon, halibut, and bottom fish. The Kodiak National Wildlife Refuge is sanctuary for many land and marine mammals in addition to the brown bear. The refuge's 800 miles of coastline supports a heavy population of waterfowl at certain times of the year in its shallows and marshes. The bald eagle lives here in such numbers that he can easily be spotted by visitors to the refuge.

If we took a giant step northwest across Shelikov Strait from Kodiak Island to the Alaska Peninsula we would make landfall in the Katmai National Park. The park encompasses 2.8 million acres of coastline spectacularly carved by bays, coves, and fjords, with high mountains in the eastern part and an interior of heavy forests and numerous lakes. Katmai was elevated to national park status in 1980, a move apparently delayed by its relative inaccessibility. The scenic, ecological, and historical values of the park may far exceed those of some of the more visited units of the system. Its most famous part, the Valley of Ten Thousand Smokes, was created in one of recorded history's most extensive volcanic eruptions, in 1912, when Novarupta, on Katmai Volcano, belched forth, with an end-of-the-world blast, 2.5 cubic miles of ash. The eruption covered a 40-square-mile area of Katmai valleys with volcanic debris, up to 700 feet deep in some places. The "ten thousand smokes" label is attributed to National Geographic Society explorers who visited Katmai in 1916, when smoke was still issuing from countless fumaroles in the valley floor. The Novarupta explosion yielded about 7 cubic miles of ash in a couple of days, much of it carried all around the Northern Hemisphere by winds.

Katmai is truly fabulous terrain for the fisherman, hiker, and backpacker. Its rivers and lakes are world-famous for rainbow, salmon, and grayling. Its mountains and valleys offer unique wilderness experiences to the explorer.

The Lake Clark region, north of Katmai and southwest of Anchorage, is another natural treasure-house of which Alaska has so many. Lake Clark, across Cook Inlet from Anchorage, is the centerpiece of Lake Clark National Park. Designated in 1980, the park is another huge one, about the size of Connecticut. With no road access to the outside, it is a complete ecological wilderness system whose integrity is preserved by its national park status. The area is well known to Alaskans, who fly in or walk in to explore its jewel-like mountain lakes, dense forests, volcanoes still spouting smoke, and a great range of big and small wildlife, including grizzly and black bears, moose, caribou, and wolves. Birds nest here in great numbers, and during migrations are even more abundant than usual.

The Matanuska Valley, northeast of Anchorage, should be included in our trip around south central Alaska. It's the richest agricultural part of the state, having more than half of Alaska's farms. It lies between the Chugach and Talkeetna mountains, and produces vegetables of heroic size during the growing season, when hours of daylight are very long. The valley shares agricultural honors to some extent with the western side of the Kenai Peninsula, where the farmland is equally fertile. The agricultural development of Matanuska Valley began in 1935 in earnest when a federally sponsored farm cooperative was launched.

Denali National Park

The single most dominant feature of the state, in the minds of Alaska residents and outsiders, surely must be that super rock of tremendous acclaim and appeal, Mount McKinley. It and its park really deserve their own chapter of commentary, but since we're trying to be orderly and parcel up the state into discrete blocks, McKinley belongs here along with its sister peaks of south central's Alaska Range. In 1980 Mount McKinley National Park was renamed Denali National Park and enlarged from 2 million acres to over 4 million acres.

Just looking at the colossal bulk of Mount McKinley from any of countless vantage points within the park where it dominates the landscape, you are tempted to wonder if you're hallucinating. It doesn't really seem possible that such a massive massif could have been pushed (and it *was* pushed) up out of the earth in one awesome piece. But there it is, and even the beautiful color studies of it in this book are not quite the same as looking at it directly. Seen, for example, from Wonder Lake, on the park road near the mountain's base, its sculptured white face is overpowering in its grandeur. One small hedge: even the grandest mountain giant is no match for a curtain of clouds, and since McKinley is fogged in about 50 percent of the time (even in summer), its appearances on center stage are often subject to the vagaries of weather.

In this century, starting in 1910, McKinley has become a much-climbed mountain. But it has always been dangerous; it has taken its toll of the ill-prepared and ill-conditioned, and sometimes the unwary have been swallowed up in its treacherous snow-covered crevasses or have simply frozen to death in the wild blizzards that roar around its twin peaks even during summer. Probably the most relaxed climb was the first, by a group of Alaskan sourdoughs who reportedly did it on a bet and very little mountaineering skill. The only mistake they made was in climbing the North Peak, a mere 19,470 feet. The true summit, the South Peak (20,320 feet) was first climbed in 1913.

Denali National Park, because it is conveniently located beside the Anchorage-Fairbanks (George Parks) Highway, is easy to get to. It has accommodations for visitors, as do all national parks, and a limited number of camping spots along the park road. Hiking, camping, and mountain climbing activities within the park all require permits, but once that is obtained, those who are wilderness-wise are in for an unforgettable experience in a unique mountain playground. The less venturesome visitor may see his scenery and wildlife from the comfort and security of a bus, on the tour that is offered from park headquarters.

The Eielson Visitor Center, 65 miles along the park road, is one of the best points on the road to see the North Peak of McKinley, just 31 miles to the southwest. The center is practically toe-to-toe with McKinley's giant Muldrow Glacier, which spreads out over the valley from the lower reaches of the mountain. Here is a good place to learn of the plant life and wildlife of the park, in talks given by park rangers. There are many grizzlies in this bear sanctuary, so numerous at Sable Pass (35-40 miles into the park) that visitors are forbidden to leave the road. There are also many other ambulatory forms of life, such as moose, caribou, Dall sheep, lynx, foxes, coyotes, beaver, squirrels, marmots, and porcupines. Among the nonambulatory life forms are aspen, birch, spruce, and willow woodlands clustered in the alpine meadows and passes.

A retinue of lesser, but still high, mountains contribute their share to the majesty of the national park. Chief among them are Mount Foraker, 17,395 feet; Mount Crosson, 12,775 feet, and Mount Silverthrone, 13,170 feet. Mount Foraker has been climbed about as much as McKinley, and is a difficult challenge for experienced alpinists.

It is, to understate things, gilding the lily to remark that south central Alaska has natural attractions that are unique in the world. It is so vast and varied that everything said about it is but a poor representation of the reality. What we would rather be saying and thinking about these priceless lands and seascapes during this time of great changes is: Go slowly—the unheeding works of one generation of men could destroy forever a host of natural wonders whose origins are older than the race of humankind.

Interior Alaska

North of the Alaska Range, south of the Brooks Range, and cut through the middle by the giant Yukon is Alaska's interior. Flowing back from the river are immense expanses of tundra, land largely unpopulated, especially to the north and west. The Yukon has three big tributaries that drain parts of the interior country: the Porcupine, flowing west out of Canada; the Tanana, heading north from the Alaska Range; and the Koyukuk, joining the Yukon where the big river drops south and west toward the Bering Sea.

The interior is not a place of great contrasts, except in temperature. In that respect it is not an accommodating place to live, having the broadest extremes in the state. The Fahrenheit readings have been 100 or more in the summer in Fort Yukon, an Indian settlement at the apex of the Yukon's arc; winter comes to Fort Yukon with great emphasis, too—the temperatures can slip into the minus 60s.

Fort Yukon is just above the Arctic Circle on the Yukon's bend. The river is about three miles wide at this point, meandering unconstrained all over the low, flat terrain, in the manner of some other Alaskan "braided" streams. This kind of behavior is typical of the river in the immense Yukon Flats region, an 80-by-250-mile basin where the Yukon sprawls in lazy abandon. In this wide, marshy plain, sand and silt brought down from glaciers by the river have been built up into islands that break the river's flow into many channels. The landscape is constantly changing under the urging of the river's many arms, but its personality remains the same. The innumerable islands are washed by inlets, bogs, swamps, sloughs and lakes. All of these characteristics contribute to making this one of the world's biggest and best waterfowl nesting grounds, offering habitat to hundreds of migratory species. Food is plentiful in the various rich aquatic environments, so the ducks and the swans and the geese and the cranes come in their millions to a bird heaven if ever there was one.

The interior has very few human inhabitants—indeed, very few settlements that could be called towns. But Alaska's second-largest city—Fairbanks—is in the heart of the heartland. Fairbanks owes its eminence to more than one cause, an important one being its situation as the northern terminus of the Alaska Highway. Four of the state's major highways meet here: the Steese, to Circle; the Elliott, to Manley Hot Springs; the Richardson, which follows the historic Abercrombie and Richardson trails through south-central Alaska; and the George Parks, the Fairbanks-Anchorage route. Fairbanks is also the northern terminus of the Alaska Railroad line, which links the two cities of Fairbanks and Anchorage, skirting the eastern boundary of Denali National Park along its route.

The Steese Highway from Fairbanks to Circle isn't very long—162 miles—but it leads through one of the most interesting regions of interior Alaska. It's not all paved and rather risky driving during the cold season. But it's the best way to cover some of this open, empty land without having to sprout wings. Because the road follows some of the old prospectors' trails, it goes through territory rich in such gold mining relics as old camps and towns, and creeks with colorful names bequeathed them by prospectors. At Eagle summit, a variety of phenomena compete for attention. Between June 20 and 22 the midnight sun may be seen from this vantage point. The caribou are partial to Eagle summit, too; it is one of their migratory routes. But one of the most spectacular summer shows in Alaska, occurring generally along the Steese, spreads out in superabundant glory at Eagle and Twelvemile summits. Everywhere along the road from late June until early August are wild flowers of every description. Alpine flora are present in multitudes: arctic forget-me-nots, alpine azalea, tall Jacob's ladder, lousewort, mountain marigolds, and many, many more.

The town of Circle lies at the end of the Steese Highway, and at the northernmost end of the interconnecting continental highway system. It is on the banks of the Yukon 50 miles south of the Arctic Circle and has only about half a hundred permanent residents. During the early trading and mining days the town was an important river port. One of the area's oddities is the hot springs located about 30 miles from Circle on a side road. Circle Hot Springs was discovered in 1893 by a prospector and now its 140-degree waters are piped into swimming pools and hot baths. An underlay of heated piping in a large garden area promotes the growth of mammoth vegetables.

The Elliott Highway, another of the interior's few roads, heads north then east from Fairbanks. Its present terminus is Manley Hot Springs, 156 miles from Fairbanks. Some day, unless further road building in Alaska is stopped, it may go to Nome, on the coast. The road offers some noteworthy views of a vast landscape with some striking natural landmarks and a profusion of wild flowers and plants. Shortly out of Fairbanks is an access point to an 80-mile hiking trail called the White Mountains Trail System. A few miles farther on, the White Mountains themselves appear. About 5,000 feet high, the white limestone ridges were named by prospectors. Because the road climbs high on the ridges and hills as it twists along its route, the views are long and spectacular. About 95 miles along the road, the flats stretch out to the south toward the Tanana River, then the foothills of the Alaska Range rise in the distance. Burned areas (from a 1968 forest fire) near the Manley end of the road are gorgeous with fireweed in July.

Manley Hot Springs is a well-manicured settlement of about 65 human inhabitants close to the Tanana River. It used to be a busy trading town during the peak of the mining days but now is a quiet, parklike little place whose residents work hard to keep it beautiful. The hot springs help it grow great swatches of green grass and splendid vegetable gardens.

Going still farther west requires an airplane or a long walk. The only village of any size between here and the coast is Tanana, an Indian town at the junction of the Tanana River with the Yukon. The town once was cheek-by-jowl with an Army post (Fort Yukon) and had an appropriately robust reputation. Today its residents lead quiet lives and make their living from trapping and fishing. The setting is beautiful, with the big river and dense forests of spruce providing the decor.

After Tanana, the great stream passes through land that is possibly the least inhabited in all the Yukon's 2,000-mile journey. The handful of villages on the river's banks as it wends its way to the coast are the only sign of humanity on the sweep of tundra plains and hills in this wilderness so typical of Alaska's heartland.

The Alaska Peninsula, The Aleutians, and The Bering Seacoast

The lower Alaska Peninsula and the Aleutian Island chain stretch so far into the North Pacific that the farthermost islands are deep into the Eastern Hemisphere. The easternmost point in the United States is not that place in Maine that keeps claiming the honor, but Pocknoi Point, on a little link in the Aleutian chain called Semisopochnoi Island. It happens to be practically touching the 180th meridian, on the *eastern* side. Another Aleutian Island, to follow the same reasoning, is the "westest" part of the United States: Amatignak Island.

The peninsula and the islands are about as thinly inhabited by people as any places on earth except the poles. But they are densely populated with wildlife of many kinds, shapes, and sizes. The Aleut (Al-ee-oot) Eskimos once had many villages on the peninsula and archipelago, but now there are very few settlements. The most noticeable human communities now are the military installations spread out along the islands. There is an abundance of bear, moose, caribou, and waterfowl living on the lower peninsula, and the whole area is sea otter territory. Except for the sea otter—now protected—the region offers hunters an amazing assortment of wild game, in season.

One especially spectacular feature of the lower Alaska Peninsula—far down on the peninsula—is the Aniakchak Crater. Its unique character geologically has entitled it to inclusion in a series of recently protected lands in Alaska. As Aniakchak National Monument, it comprises a whole ecosystem of 440,000 acres. The crater rim is six miles in diameter, more than 4,000 feet above sea level. The crater contains a lake within its 30 square miles, a lake whose waters find egress through a 2,000-foot cleft in the rim and flow as the Aniakchak River 27 miles to the sea. Some phenomena of the Aniakchak area are cinder cones and warm springs, abundant big and small wildlife—especially bears, and a succession of plant life.

Some 250 miles north of the Fox Islands (a group in the middle of the Aleutian chain), are the Pribilofs. These little islands in the Bering Sea are most noteworthy as a fur seal rookery. The Pribilof wildlife—seals and the seabirds—have little fear of man, and visitors can get quite close for picture-taking purposes. Besides cameras, visitors might do well to bring along some ear plugs. Between the barking and roaring of the male seals during mating season and the raucous cries of the birds, the din is usually well above what is permitted by noise ordinances in the lower 49. Many varieties of subarctic flora also grow on the Pribilofs.

Bristol Bay reaches inland 200 miles between the Alaska Peninsula and the southwest mainland coast of Alaska. The bay is 270 miles wide at its mouth and opens onto the Bering Sea. Most of the world's sockeye salmon come from here, from the waters of the bay and the canneries on its shores.

After Bristol Bay, Western Alaska begins in earnest, a region that few Alaskans ever see. It's flatland that stretches over immense distances of treeless tundra, from Bristol Bay north around the Seward Peninsula to the Arctic Circle. Hundreds of thousands of lakes, ponds, and sloughs cut up the land. Two great river deltas meander to the sea in countless streams—the Kuskokwim, emptying into Kuskokwim Bay; and the mighty Yukon, which finally ends its journey across Yukon Territory and Alaska about 150 miles north at Norton Sound. There's a scattering of Eskimo villages across this vast wilderness, in places where fishing and trapping are still the main livelihood. Western Alaska is a place of high winds in the winter and rainy, cool summery weather.

The government has established several protected areas for wildlife in this region as in other parts of Alaska. Nunivak Island, about 20 miles off the coast in the Bering Sea, is one of these. It is a refuge for the musk ox, reduced now to one herd in the United States.

The tiny settlements of this coast have economies based on fisheries in some form, and on hunting to some extent. Traditional arts and crafts of the Eskimo are practiced and maintained, both as for the sake of cultural continuity and for additional income from sales of the articles created. The big towns of western Alaska are Bethel and Nome, both with about 2,500 inhabitants. Bethel, because of its location near the mouth of the Kuskokwim River, is headquarters for the huge Clarence Rhode Wildlife Refuge in the Yukon-Kuskokwim River deltas—possibly the greatest waterfowl breeding ground in the world. Fishing, hunting, and tourism contribute to Bethel's economy. Air tours of the tundra and village areas around Bethel are organized here for visitors.

Nome is on the south shore of Seward Peninsula. It is the best known town in western Alaska, because of its gold rush history that began at the end of the 19th century. It was called Anvil City at first, after a creek by that name where the first gold strike was made. In 1889 gold was discovered in the beach sand of Nome, and the race was on. Nome's population boomed to 30,000 during this period.

Nome faces the sometimes furious Bering Sea, at the mouth of Norton Sound. Front Street is right at the water's edge, and a high sea wall of boulders lines one side of the street to protect the town from the unchecked wrath of storms that blow in from the sea. Nome is really an Arctic town, although not officially in the Arctic Zone. It has that long arctic summer day and that dark, long winter night. It is the takeoff point, by air, for other, more northerly places with harsher climates, inhabited mostly by Eskimos.

Brush Alaska, as these outlying areas are called, is hospitable to the intrepid visitor who adapts himself to its life style. The only access to villages like Gambell, Savoonga, and Wales is by air from Nome. Teller is on the Nome-Teller road, so is more accessible. But the more remote places naturally offer a more profound experience of the Eskimo people and their ways, especially if the outsider is invited to stay with an Eskimo family and is not averse to eating wild foods, like sea lion, muktuk, and caribou. Even here, traditional ways of life are changing, now that Alaska is more and more the focus of man's desperate search for new sources of energy. But for now and the near future, the Eskimos of the tundra country are an example, to more technologically dependent societies, of the satisfactory life available to those who contend successfully with the harsher aspects of nature.

Arctic Alaska

Arctic Alaska is another one of those complex worlds within the already complicated "Great Land." It's not just a flat frozen expanse relieved only by an occasional Eskimo fishing through a hole in the ice. But it is quite sharply delineated as a discrete region by mighty mountain barriers, primarily the Brooks Range—an enormous and intricate jumble of ridges that stretches across all the north land and spawns some giant rivers whose waters flow down the Arctic Slope to the Arctic Ocean some 200 miles away. The northern tip is Point Barrow, 1,300 miles from the North Pole.

This is a land of permafrost, meaning that the ground is frozen year-round, with only a few inches of thin top soil yielding to the summer's sun's comparative warmth. The innumerable ponds and lakes of the Arctic are the result of collected water runoff from snowmelt. The water stays above ground because it cannot penetrate the frozen ground.

To look at its strange and varied landscapes we might begin on the west coast, on the north shore of Kotzebue Sound. About 35 miles northwest of the Eskimo village of Kotzebue is Cape Krusenstern National Monument, where beach ridges hold a treasurehouse of archaeological evidence indicative of almost every culturally distinct period since man began his move into the north American continent. Artifacts found in these beach ridges go back 5,000 years and more.

Kotzebue is perched on the Baldwin Peninsula, a skinny splotch of land that juts out into Kotzebue Sound opposite the site of the Noatak River's outlet into the sound. The Eskimo village is also near the mouth of the Kobuk River. Both of these streams are big, wild watercourses that drain mountainous terrain of surpassing beauty and strange phenomena. They are both included in wilderness protected lands: the Kobuk Valley National Park and the Noatak National Preserve. The Kobuk Valley includes 1.8 million acres along the river featuring the Great Kobuk Sand Dunes, 25 square miles of puzzles to anyone who expects nothing but snow and ice above the Arctic Circle. The valley is also rich in archaeological finds, evidences of early cultures like those found at Cape Krusenstern, but arranged in vertical strata instead of horizontally, as they are at the cape. This is the crossroads of the Asiatic-North American Flyway, and a great many species of birds are found in the valley. Some 31 kinds of mammalian life, including caribou, roam the Kobuk Valley at some time during the year.

One of the priceless resources of Arctic Alaska is the Noatak River basin. It is still in a pristine state—one of the very few large and significant unspoiled areas left in the world. Thus the authorization just mentioned, of the Noatak National Preserve. The Noatak is not spectacular mountain country, except where the river rises in the central Brooks Range, but it has an awesome sweep, an openness that is associated with Great Plains country, or desert. The Noatak is 450 miles long and courses through a variety of landscapes before emptying into Kotzebue Sound. Its original source is the glaciers of Mount Igikpak (8,520 feet); it is also fed by ten tributary rivers, numerous creeks, and uncounted lakes scattered through the basin. The upper Noatak country is a deep valley. Farther downstream the river wanders across a vast plain bordered on the north by the De Long Mountains and by the Baird Mountains on the south. But the mountains are so distant in this wide part of the valley they appear as insignificant blue hills. About halfway along its career the river cuts into 70-mile-long Noatak Canyon, where scattered spruce trees first appear, gradually becoming more numerous as the river leaves the canyon and splits into many channels in its trip through a five-mile-wide valley. This region is particularly ideal for waterfowl habitat, with its many ponds and sloughs.

The river passes Noatak Village, the only settlement in the basin, within 70 miles of the sea. After passing through the Igichuk Hills the Noatak enters its delta and empties into Kotzebue Sound. This unique river basin is the largest in this nation still unaltered by man. It is hard to believe that it will long remain so.

Up and around the northwest coast, human habitations are almost as rare as palm trees (or *any* trees). Two settlements are Point Hope, on a finger of land that stands out into the Chukchi Sea; and Barrow, near the point which juts into the Arctic Ocean. Point Hope's Eskimo residents (400) are great whale hunters—the village's situation near deep water brings the giant mammals close to shore. The village is also the site of Eskimo cultures of former times, and archaeologists are working there. Barrow is the largest Eskimo village in the world, and, although modern in the 20th-century sense, is also quite dependent on whale hunting for its livelihood. A portent of the future may be indicated by the fact that many of the homes there are heated by natural gas from nearby fields.

In the center of Arctic Alaska, and in the central Brooks Range, is Anaktuvuk Pass. It is both a pass and a native village, at the heart of the north slope wilderness whose forbidding climate has so far acted as a protective shield and left it largely unexplored. Of course, as most people know who follow the oil pipeline activities in Alaska, the Brooks Range was breached at Anaktuvuk in 1968 by a "haul road" to

Prudhoe Bay and Arctic oil fields, and later by the oil pipeline itself, east of the pass. Except for these tiny incursions by man, the Brooks Range remains inviolate, much as it was 45 years ago when the explorer Robert Marshall wrote about its wonders. It's another of Alaska's pristine lands that the world is beginning to look on with both worried and covetous eyes. The worry comes from the conservationists; the coveters are folks of many different backgrounds who regard virgin land as prime territory for exploitation of some kind.

The federal government has already given some attention to proposals for protecting this wilderness. Gates of the Arctic National Park was established in 1980. The so-called Gates of Arctic, jagged, granite spires in the east-central Brooks Range, is the centerpiece of a park that includes pristine lakes, braided rivers, and tundra, plus the still more spectacular and craggy Arrigetch Peaks to the west. The native village at Anaktuvuk is the only habitation in this immense, harsh environment. Wild storms and cold bite down on the winter landscape, but many kinds of life have adapted to it—the region is bursting with life. Vast, yawning space and fragile life forms seem paradoxical, but here in the brief summer the tundra glows with multicolored wild flowers. As a wilderness recreation area, its use by people is strictly controlled. Perhaps nowhere else in Alaska is the quality of the wilderness experience so dependent on limited use. The "Gates" region is above all a fragile ecosystem where recovery is close to impossible once damage has been done. The mountain passes here are pathways for the spring and fall migrations of the 240,000-strong Arctic caribou herd.

One minus for the oil pipeline is already obvious, however. (The recently completed line crosses the caribou route, although it is not believed to be any obstacle to the herds because of being elevated where it crosses migration pathways.) Many of the scars left in this delicate tundra land by the heavy equipment used in the construction of that pipeline will become more pronounced as time goes on. Erosive consequences gain the upper hand where the terrain is under the dominion of such a terribly stern weather regime.

Farther south, but still considered part of Arctic Alaska, is the region where the Porcupine River joins the upper Yukon as it bends northward early on its trip through Alaska. The settlement of Fort Yukon, on its namesake river near the confluence, was once a trading post of the Hudson's Bay Company. A point of pride with the few hundred Fort Yukon residents (Athabascan Indians) are the exuberant summer gardens produced here, encouraged by what seems an impossible weather situation so far north: the summertime temperature has been recorded at 100 degrees. The Athasbascans are exceptionally skilled in beadwork, selling beadwork moccasins and other clothing articles made from moose and caribou hides tanned by the Indian women.